Contents

How to Use This Book

Numbers and Operations helps your learner build a strong foundation in fourth-grade number relations skills. The identification and manipulation of numbers are essential building blocks for later mathematical studies. Through engaging activities based on academic standards set by the National Council of Teachers of Mathematics (NCTM), *Numbers and Operations* provides your learner with the practice he or she needs to build confidence in working with numbers.

This Brain Builders activity book features six sections, each highlighting a different aspect of the fourth-grade math curriculum. Each section presents four curriculum-based activities. These activities offer easy-to-follow directions as well as skill definitions and examples. Many of the activities also feature kid-friendly fun facts related to the subject matter, designed to show learners how math exists in the world around them.

Whole Number Concepts
The first section of this book focuses on ordering and comparing numbers, recognizing prime numbers, expressing numerals in word form, and expanded notation.

Number Sense
The second section of this book involves place value and rounding. Learners are presented with a variety of activities that prompt them to apply their knowledge of place value up to the millions place.

Addition and Subtraction
The third section of this book concentrates on addition and subtraction. Through basic problems and word problems, learners strengthen their knowledge of these core skills.

Multiplication and Division

The fourth section of this book develops learners' abilities in solving multiplication and division problems. As learners work with basic and word problems, they use both their computational and analytical skills.

Fractions

The fifth section of this book focuses on fractions. Learners explore different ways of representing and manipulating fractions as they identify equivalent fractions, recognize representations of fractions, and add and subtract fractions with like denominators.

Decimals

The sixth section of this book involves decimals. Activities prompt learners to compare, add, subtract, and relate decimals to equivalent fractions.

Skills Correlation Guide

	Ordering and Comparing	Prime Numbers	Expanded Notation	Numerals in Word Form	Place Value	Rounding	Addition	Subtraction	Word Problems	Factors	Multiplication	Division	Representations	Equivalent Fractions
Whole Number Concepts (pp. 11–15)	✓	✓	✓	✓										
Number Sense (pp. 17–21)					✓	✓								
Addition and Subtraction (pp. 23–27)							✓	✓	✓					
Multiplication and Division (pp. 29–33)									✓	✓	✓	✓		
Fractions (pp. 35–39)							✓	✓					✓	
Decimals (pp. 41–45)	✓						✓	✓						✓

The activities featured in this book are level R according to the guidelines set by Fountas and Pinnell.

Name _____

Ordering and Comparing Numbers

 Directions: Write each set of numbers in order from least to greatest on the lines below.

1. 5,691   962   13,028   426

_____

2. 9,720   10,485   658   219

_____

3. 7,509   397   6,999   10,001

_____

4. 19,452   868   8,091   1,304

_____

4

Name _____

Rounding

 Directions: Follow the directions below and write your answers on the lines provided.

1. Round 13,789 to the nearest hundreds place.

   _____

2. Round 1,748 to the nearest thousands place.

   _____

3. Round 32,961 to the nearest ten thousands place.

   _____

4. Round 9,083 to the nearest tens place.

   _____

Name _____

Addition

 Directions: Add each group of numbers below.

1.
$$
\begin{array}{r}
809 \\
430 \\
+\ 628 \\
\hline
\end{array}
$$

2.
$$
\begin{array}{r}
761 \\
308 \\
249 \\
+\ 800 \\
\hline
\end{array}
$$

3.
$$
\begin{array}{r}
991 \\
351 \\
388 \\
748 \\
+\ 529 \\
\hline
\end{array}
$$

4.
$$
\begin{array}{r}
537 \\
301 \\
128 \\
452 \\
+\ 206 \\
\hline
\end{array}
$$

6

Division with Remainders

 Directions: Solve each problem below.

1. 41 ÷ 5 = _____   Remainder _____

2. 31 ÷ 3 = _____   Remainder _____

3. 17 ÷ 2 = _____   Remainder _____

4. 21 ÷ 8 = _____   Remainder _____

Name _____

Fractions

Recognizing Fractions

 Directions: On the lines below, write the fraction equal to the shaded part of each picture.

1. 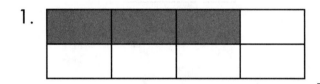 _____

2. 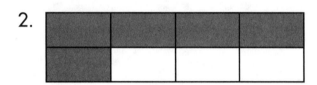 _____

3. 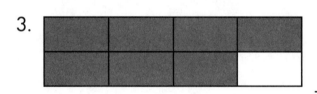 _____

4. 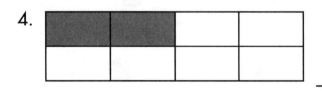 _____

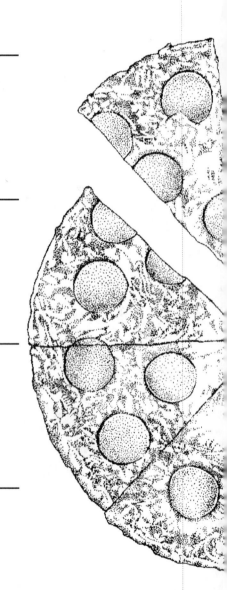

8

Name _____

Comparing Decimals

 Directions: Write >, <, or = in each box to complete each number sentence.

1. 5.09 ☐ 50.9

2. 4.1 ☐ 4.10

3. 13 ☐ 0.13

4. 8.71 ☐ 87.1

Teaching Tips...

For *Whole Number Concepts*
(pp. 11–15)

- **Background**
  In this section, learners work with several whole number concepts. Using their reasoning abilities, learners compare and order whole numbers, recognize prime numbers, express numbers in expanded notation, and write numbers in word form.

- **Homework Helper**
  For a lesson in real-world math, have learners write checks for things they would like to buy. This activity offers learners extra practice in writing numbers in word form.

- **Research-based Activity**
  Have learners do research in the library or on the Internet to see how a checking account works. After they have completed their research, ask learners to write a paragraph describing what they have discovered.

- **Test Prep**
  Understanding whole number concepts is important for building a foundation for higher math. The skills featured in this section frequently appear on standardized tests.

- **Different Audiences**
  Help learners for whom English is a second language (ESL) master the skills in this section with flash cards. Write the word form of a numeral on one side of each card and the numeral on the other side. Allow the learners to use these cards to complete assignments until they are more comfortable with the language.

- **Group Activity**
  Divide learners into several groups. Give each group a topic, such as roller coasters, mountains, bridges, or buildings. Ask each group to do research to find the five largest examples of their assigned topic. Have the groups compare the sizes, listing them in ascending and descending order.

TEACHING TIPS

10

Name _____

Out of Order!

Numbers can be arranged by their value, either from greatest to least or from least to greatest.

Example: The numbers 43,290; 2,973; 983; and 4,265 listed in order from least to greatest are: 983; 2,973; 4,265; and 43,290.

 Directions: Write each set of numbers in order from least to greatest on the lines below.

1. 1,236   2,694   190   782   974 _____

_____

2. 1,090   564   1,468   294   985 _____

_____

3. 651   2,012   10,004   97   512 _____

_____

4. 3,450   596   396   1,678   20,546 _____

_____

FUN FACT

Listed in order from greatest to least, the world's three tallest towers are the Petronas Towers (1,483 feet or 452.02 meters), the Empire State Building (1,454 feet or 443.18 m), and the Sears Tower (1,450 feet or 441.96 m).

11

Name _____

Prime Puzzlers

A prime number is a whole number that is greater than 1 and can only be equally divided by 1 and itself.

Example: The number 7 is a prime number. It can only be equally divided by 1 and 7.

 Directions: Circle each prime number and the letter below it. Cross out all of the other numbers and letters to read the answer to the riddle.

RIDDLE: Name a table that you don't learn in math class.

14	13	26	29	2	24	19	15	17	18	11
G	D	O	I	N	H	N	A	E	T	R

19	16	3	7	0	5	22	31	27
T	B	A	B	W	L	N	E	D

FUN FACT
Currently, the largest known prime number is 6,320,430 digits long!

Name _____

Expanding Numbers

We can expand numbers to show the place value of each digit.
Example: To expand the number 123, we write 100 + 20 + 3. This shows that
the digit 1 is in the hundreds place, the digit 2 is in the tens place,
and the digit 3 is in the ones place.

 Directions: Circle the correct expanded form of each number.

1. 425

   A. 4 + 2 + 5   B. 40 + 20 + 5

   C. 400 + 20 + 5

2. 5,906

   A. 500 + 90 + 6   B. 5,000 + 900 + 6

   C. 5,000 + 900 + 60

3. 3,861

   A. 3,000 + 800 + 61   B. 3,000 + 800 + 60 + 1

   C. 3,000 + 800 + 60 + 10

4. 12,308

   A. 10,000 + 2,000 + 300 + 80   B. 1,000 + 2,000 + 300 + 8

   C. 10,000 + 2,000 + 300 + 8

FUN FACT

**Expand means to become larger or longer. Expanding a
number is writing it out in a longer form.**

Name _____

Writing Numbers as Words

Numbers can be written as words.

Example: The number 422 can be written as four hundred twenty-two.

 Directions: Write each number in words on the lines below.

1. 32 _____

2. 145 _____

3. 604 _____

4. 1,165 _____

FUN FACT

We write numbers as words on checks.

Name _____

Skill Check—Whole Number Concepts

Ordering and Comparing Numbers

 Directions: Write the numbers in order from least to greatest.

1,093   983   10,211   519

_____

Recognizing Prime Numbers

 Directions: Circle the prime numbers below.

18   2   11   13   6

Expanding Numbers

 Directions: Write 4,762 in expanded form.

_____

Numerals in Word Form

 Directions: Write the number 845 in words.

_____

Teaching Tips...

TEACHING TIPS

- **Background**
  In this section, learners work with the place value of digits as they round whole numbers to the nearest ten, hundred, thousand, ten thousand, and hundred thousand. Each activity focuses on strengthening the learner's ability to recognize place value and round accordingly.

- **Homework Helper**
  Provide learners with two lists of numbers. The first list should have rounded numbers and the second list should have exact numbers. Have learners time themselves while finding the sum of each list of numbers. Next, have learners compare the amount of time it took them to add up each list. Explain that the sum of rounded numbers can often be found more quickly, hence the use of estimation in everyday life.

- **Research-based Activity**
  Have learners research the population of major cities. Have them write a paragraph detailing their findings. Ask learners to explain why population numbers are rounded numbers.

- **Test Prep**
  In this section, learners gain valuable practice in making sense of numbers. As they broaden this sense, learners become better prepared for classroom math tests.

- **Different Audiences**
  Help a challenged learner master rounding numbers by drawing a number line. A number line, a visual representation of numbers listed in order on a line, can serve as a helpful tool. Learners can use the line to decide whether to round a number up or down.

- **Group Activity**
  Give groups of learners different colored blocks. Assign each color a different place value. Give groups several different numbers to represent using the blocks. For example, the color red might represent the ones place and the color blue might represent the tens place. To represent the number 21, a group would line up one red block and two blue blocks.

16

Name _____

What's Its Value?

A digit is any one of the ten symbols 0, 1, 2, 3, 4, 5, 6, 7, 8, or 9 used to write numbers. Place value is the value of a single digit depending on its place in a number.

Example: The value of the digit 7 in the number 357,209 is 7,000.

 Directions: Find the value of the digit 5 in each number. Write each value on the line provided.

1. 504,297 _____

2. 1,305,162 _____

3. 5,234,007 _____

4. 496,052 _____

FUN FACT

An Australian man named *Les Stewart* once typed out each number from 1 to 1,000,000 using his typewriter. It took him 16 years to do it!

17

Name _____

Digit Value

A digit is any one of the ten symbols 0, 1, 2, 3, 4, 5, 6, 7, 8, or 9 used to write numbers. Place value is the value of a single digit depending on its place in a number.

Example: In the number 14,270,980, the digit 4 is in the millions place.

 Directions: Look at the number below. Write the digit that is in each place listed.

128,239

1. tens place _____

2. hundred thousands place _____

3. thousands place _____

4. ones place _____

FUN FACT

The number listed above—128,239—is the weight (in pounds) of the largest cake ever made!

Name _____

Rounding Up and Down

To round a number is to increase or decrease that number to the nearest 10, 100, 1000, and so on. To round the number 34,809 to the nearest thousand we first find the digit in the thousands place. That digit is 4. Next, we look at the digit one place to the right of the 4. That digit, 8, is in the hundreds place. Since 8 is greater than 5, we change the 4 in the thousands place to a 5 and change each digit to the right of that digit to a 0. Therefore, 34,809 rounded to the nearest thousand is 35,000.

 Directions: Follow the directions below. Write your answers on the lines provided.

1. Round 204,561 to the nearest hundreds place. _____

2. Round 5,291 to the nearest thousands place. _____

3. Round 4,293,099 to the nearest hundred thousands place. _____

4. Round 490,621 to the nearest tens place. _____

FUN FACT
If you rounded a number to the nearest trillion, there would be 12 zeros.

Name _____

Which Place Is It?

To round a number is to increase or decrease that number to the nearest 10, 100, 1000, and so on. To find the place to which a number has been rounded, find the digit in the number farthest to the right that is greater than 0. That digit is in the place to which the number has been rounded.

Example: To find the place that 45,900 has been rounded to, we find the digit farthest to the right that is greater than 0. That digit, 9, is in the hundreds place, therefore the number has been rounded to the hundreds place.

 Directions: Find the place to which each number has been rounded. Write your answers on the lines below.

1. 14,000 _____

2. 620 _____

3. 980,000 _____

4. 1,256,400 _____

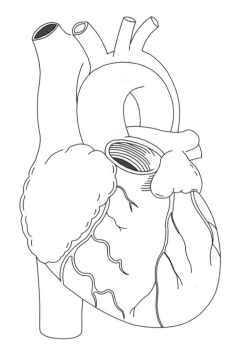

FUN FACT

The human heart beats around 100,000 times each day. This number has been rounded to the hundred thousands place.

Name _____

Skill Check—Number Sense

Place Value

 Directions: Answer the questions below.

1. What is the value of the digit 2 in the number 63,213?

   _____

2. What digit is in the thousands place in the number 48,309?

   _____

Rounding

 Directions: Answer the questions below.

1. What is 5,926 rounded to the hundreds place?

   _____

2. To what place has the number 2,354,000 been rounded?

   _____

21

Teaching Tips...

For *Addition and Subtraction*
(pp. 23–27)

- **Background**

  This section features a variety of addition and subtraction problems. In the following activities, learners demonstrate basic addition and subtraction skills as well as their abilities to solve addition and subtraction word problems.

- **Homework Helper**

  Have learners practice rounding while solving addition problems. Before doing a basic addition problem, have learners round the numbers to a set place value. Have learners find the sums of the original numbers and the rounded numbers. Next, have learners find the difference between the two sums to see how accurate rounding actually is.

- **Research-based Activity**

  Have learners interview their family members about their respective ages. Ask learners to find the sum of all of the ages.

- **Test Prep**

  Addition and subtraction are the building blocks of elementary math skills. Practice in this area will help learners succeed on both classroom and standardized tests.

- **Different Audiences**

  Have an accelerated learner write his or her own word problems and solve them. Ask the learner to look for inspiration in his or her everyday life. This will challenge the learner's imagination and increase his or her proficiency in addition and subtraction.

- **Group Activity**

  Separate learners into groups of two. Have each group create a worksheet and an answer key with ten addition and subtraction problems. Next, have the groups exchange worksheets with one another for homework. The next day, learners can grade each other's papers and discuss any wrong answers.

Name _____

Add It Up!

To add two numbers is to join them together to find a sum, or total amount.

Example:
```
   456
 + 537
   993
```

 Directions: Solve each problem below.

1.
```
   742
   458
 + 294
```

2.
```
   851
   622
 + 909
```

3.
```
   621
   809
   353
   468
 + 157
```

4.
```
   461
   834
   272
   655
 + 781
```

FUN FACT
An average pencil can write about 50,000 words.

Name _____

Let's Subtract!

To subtract is to find out how much is left over after taking one number away from another number.

Example:
$$\begin{array}{r} 475 \\ -\ 245 \\ \hline 230 \end{array}$$

 Directions: Solve each problem below.

1. $\begin{array}{r} 789 \\ -\ 203 \\ \hline \end{array}$

2. $\begin{array}{r} 278 \\ -\ 159 \\ \hline \end{array}$

3. $\begin{array}{r} 623 \\ -\ 482 \\ \hline \end{array}$

4. $\begin{array}{r} 501 \\ -\ 299 \\ \hline \end{array}$

FUN FACT

When a number is subtracted from a smaller number, the result is called a negative number. Negative numbers are less than zero.

24

Name _____

Real-World Math

We can use addition and subtraction to solve real-world math problems.
Example: Nelson had 143 marbles in his bag. He dropped the bag and some
fell out. Now Nelson only has 106 marbles in his bag. How many
marbles did he lose?   143 – 106 = 37. Nelson lost 37 marbles.

 **Directions: Solve the following word problems. Write your
answers on the lines provided.**

1. Anne is shopping for clothes. She has $150 to spend. Anne wants a dress
   that costs $50, a shirt that costs $35, and a jacket that costs $40. Does
   Anne have enough money to buy the clothes she wants?

   _____

2. Tim had $85. Then he bought a pair of sneakers that cost $55 and a book
   that cost $13. How much money does Tim have left?

   _____

3. Jack and his family are going to Florida. They have to travel 752 miles to get
   there. So far, they have gone 426 miles. How many more miles do they
   have to travel?

   _____

4. All of the students and teachers at the Fostertown Elementary School are
   going to see a show in a theater. The theater has 400 seats. There are 372
   students and 32 teachers at the school. Are there enough seats for everyone?

   _____

Name _____

Addition and Subtraction Word Problems

We can use addition and subtraction to solve real-world math problems.
Example: Cindy wants to buy three compact discs. They cost $18, $21, and $12. How much do the three compact discs cost in total?
$18 + $21 + $12 = $51

  **Directions: Solve the following word problems and write your answers on the lines provided.**

1. Christine is buying some books for her vacation. The books cost $19, $24, and $12. If Christine has $65, does she have enough money to buy all three books?

   _____

2. Geeta is throwing a party. She spends $346 on food, $102 on decorations, and $54 on music. How much money does Geeta spend in total?

   _____

3. Shawn has $168 to spend on DVD sets of his favorite television shows. The sets he wants cost $48, $109, and $39. Does Shawn have enough money to buy all of the DVD sets he wants?

   _____

4. Marcos is saving money to buy a car. He saved $405 in January, $352 in February, and $269 in March. How much has Marcos saved so far?

26

   _____

Name _____

Skill Check—Addition and Subtraction

Addition and Subtraction Problems

 Directions: Solve each problem below.

1.
```
  562
  253
  395
+ 159
─────
```

2.
```
  903
- 287
─────
```

Addition and Subtraction Word Problems

 Directions: Solve each problem below.

1. Diane collects stickers. In one sticker book, she has 215 stickers, in another book she has 309 stickers, and in a third book, she has 197 stickers. How many stickers does Diane have in her collection?

   _____

2. Rasheed had 250 candy bars to sell. On Monday, he sold 67 candy bars. On Tuesday, he sold 42 candy bars. Today, Rasheed sold 72 candy bars. How many candy bars does Rasheed have left to sell?

   _____

Teaching Tips...

- ## Background
  Multiplication and division skills are essential to mastering elementary school mathematics. In this section, learners gain valuable practice in factor recognition, solving basic multiplication and division problems, and solving word problems involving multiplication and division.

- ## Homework Helper
  Have learners create posters of a multiplication table for the numbers 0 through 12. Encourage them to be creative with color and design. Display the finished tables for everyone to see.

- ## Research-based Activity
  The multiplication table has been used for many years. Have learners research archaeological discoveries of ancient multiplication tables and write a paragraph about what they have discovered.

- ## Test Prep
  Learners develop essential skills in this section, including recognizing factors, finding remainders, and solving word problems. These skills frequently appear on standardized tests.

- ## Different Audiences
  Help a challenged learner understand multiplication and division by using visual representations of problems. Use groups of nuts, grapes, or other small objects to show the challenged learner how multiplication and division are based on the bringing together and separating of groups.

- ## Group Activity
  Play multiplication and division bingo with a group of learners. Hand out bingo cards and instead of calling numbers, call multiplication or division problems. The answers to the problems should reflect the numbers on the cards. Learners can mark their cards as they correctly solve problems. The first one to successfully get a BINGO wins.

Name _____

Fun with Factors

A factor is a whole number that can be divided equally into another number.
Example: 1, 2, and 4 are factors of 4.

 Directions: Follow the directions below.

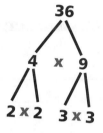

1. Write all of the factors of 32 on the line.

_____

2. Circle the numbers below that are not factors of 20.

   1   2   3   4   5   7   9   10   12

3. Write all the factors of 16 on the line.

_____

4. Circle the numbers below that are not factors of 12.

   12   3   5   6   1   9   2   10   4

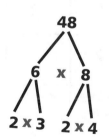

FUN FACT

Of the numbers 1 through 20, the number 12 has the most factors. It has six: 1, 2, 3, 4, 6, and 12.

29

Name _____

Multiplication Tables

Multiplication is a process in which a number is added to itself a certain number of times.

Example: 2 x 4 = 8 is the same as adding 2 + 2 + 2 + 2 = 8

 Directions: Fill in the multiplication table below. One of the boxes has been filled in for you.

	5	9	2	7	10
4					
1					
6					
8			16		
3					
7					
9					
5					
2					

FUN FACT

Clay multiplication tables that are more than 3,000 years old have been found in different parts of the world.

Name _____

How Much Remains?

Sometimes a number cannot be divided equally into another number. The amount that is left over is called the remainder.

Example: We cannot divide 7 by 2 equally. There is a remainder left over.

$7 \div 2 = 3$, with a remainder of 1.

 Directions: Solve each problem below.

1. $32 \div 7 =$ _____   Remainder _____

2. $25 \div 4 =$ _____   Remainder _____

3. $16 \div 5 =$ _____   Remainder _____

4. $11 \div 2 =$ _____   Remainder _____

FUN FACT

The word *remain* means to be left over.

31

Name _____

Word Problems

We can use multiplication and division to solve real-world word problems.
Example: Sonya baked 24 cookies. She wants to give an even number of cookies
to each of her four brothers. How many cookies does each of Sonya's
brothers receive?   24 ÷ 4 = 6 They received 6 cookies each.

 **Directions: Solve each problem below and write your answer
on the line provided.**

1. Today is Jake's birthday. There are 5 relatives in Jake's family. Each of his
   relatives gives Jake $9. How much money does Jake receive in all?

   _____

2. Louis is putting his baseball cards into a book. Each page of
   the book can hold 4 cards. If Louis has 23 cards, how many
   pages can he fill? How many cards will he have left over?

   _____

3. Sheena is planting tomatoes in her garden. She plants 6
   rows of tomatoes with 9 plants in each row. How many
   tomato plants does Sheena have in all?

   _____

4. Chrissy has 32 pieces of candy. She wants to give each of her 8 friends an
   equal amount of candy. How many pieces of candy does each of Chrissy's
   friends receive?

© Rosen School Supply•Brain Builders Numbers and Operations•4•RSS-8574-1

Name _____

Skill Check—Multiplication and Division

Recognizing Factors

 Directions: Circle the numbers that are factors of 24.

3, 4, 5, 8, 10, 12, 2, 1, 6, 7

Multiplication Tables

 Directions: Fill in the multiplication table.

	0	8	5
11			
4			

Division with Remainders

 Directions: Solve the problem below.

1. 19 ÷ 3 = _____   Remainder _____

2. 27 ÷ 5 = _____   Remainder _____

Teaching Tips...

• Background

In this section, learners practice working with fractions and mixed numbers. The activities involve recognizing fractions as pictures, working with equivalent fractions, and adding and subtracting fractions with like denominators.

• Homework Helper

Give learners a set number of beans in a variety of colors. Have them write fractions that represent the relationship between each color bean and the total number of beans.

• Research-based Activity

Have learners keep a fraction journal in which they record each time they encounter a fraction in their everyday lives. For example, a learner might record eating a slice of pizza ($\frac{1}{8}$), eating a section of an orange ($\frac{1}{6}$), or the amount of a book they might have read ($\frac{2}{3}$).

• Test Prep

Curriculum requirements for elementary math stipulate that learners should be comfortable working with basic fractions and mixed numbers at this level. Classroom and standardized tests frequently measure learners' proficiency in this area.

• Different Audiences

Explore the use of fractional language with a learner for whom English is a second language (ESL). Help that learner identify the many ways fractions are used in the English language. For example, introduce the learner to the terms half-past, halfway, quarter, etc.

• Group Activity

Break learners into several large groups. Have the groups figure out what fraction of them are wearing sneakers, belts, or T-shirts. Have groups compare their findings.

Name _____

Picture It!

A fraction is a number that names a part of a whole or a part of a group. A mixed number is a whole number plus a fraction.

Examples:

 This picture shows the fraction $\frac{3}{4}$.

 This picture shows the mixed number $1\frac{1}{2}$.

 Directions: On the line provided, write the fraction or mixed number shown in each picture.

1. _____

2. _____

3. _____

4. 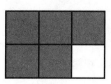 _____

Name _____

Different Fractions, Same Amount

Equivalent fractions are fractions that name the same amount.

Example: $\frac{2}{4}$ and $\frac{1}{2}$ are equivalent fractions because they both name the same amount.

$\frac{2}{4}$ = $\frac{1}{2}$

 Directions: Write an equivalent fraction for each fraction on the lines below. Draw pictures on a separate sheet of paper to help you.

1. $\frac{2}{8}$ _____

2. $\frac{3}{9}$ _____

3. $\frac{6}{12}$ _____

4. $\frac{3}{15}$ _____

FUN FACT
The word equivalent means equal.

Name _____

Fractions with Like Denominators

Fraction Fun

The top part of a fraction is called the numerator. The bottom part of the fraction is called the denominator. We can add fractions with like denominators by adding the numerators together.

Example: $\frac{1}{8} + \frac{2}{8} = \frac{3}{8}$

 Directions: Add the following fractions. Write your answers on the lines below.

1. $\frac{2}{8} + \frac{5}{8}$ = _____

2. $\frac{1}{5} + \frac{3}{5}$ = _____

3. $\frac{5}{16} + \frac{2}{16}$ = _____

4. $\frac{8}{11} + \frac{2}{11}$ = _____

FUN FACT

The denominator of a fraction tells how many parts there are. The numerator tells how many parts of the whole are *being* talked about.

37

Name _____

Fractions with Like Denominators

Fraction Subtraction

The top part of a fraction is called the numerator. The bottom part of the fraction is called the denominator. We can subtract fractions with like denominators. We subtract the smaller numerator from the larger numerator to find the difference between the fractions.

Example: $\dfrac{5}{8} - \dfrac{4}{8} = \dfrac{1}{8}$

 Directions: Subtract the following fractions. Write your answers on the lines below.

1. $\dfrac{7}{8} - \dfrac{2}{8} =$ _____

2. $\dfrac{6}{11} - \dfrac{3}{11} =$ _____

3. $\dfrac{12}{13} - \dfrac{7}{13} =$ _____

4. $\dfrac{8}{9} - \dfrac{4}{9} =$ _____

FUN FACT

Fractions can be found in recipe books. Ingredient lists often ask for $\dfrac{1}{2}$ cup of sugar or $\dfrac{3}{4}$ cup of flour.

38

Name _____

Skill Check—Fractions

Identifying Representations

 Directions: Write the fraction shown in this picture.

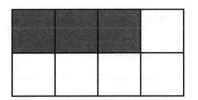 _____

Equivalent Fractions

 Directions: Write an equivalent fraction for the fraction below.

$\frac{2}{12}$ _____

Fractions with Like Denominators

 Directions: Solve the following problems.

1. $\frac{4}{9} + \frac{3}{9} =$ _____

2. $\frac{9}{11} - \frac{6}{11} =$ _____

39

Teaching Tips...

• Background

Decimals are an integral part of elementary mathematics. As learners develop an understanding of decimal values, they broaden their comprehension of fractions and place value. In this section, learners will compare decimals, add and subtract decimals, and find fractional equivalents of decimals.

• Homework Helper

Have learners write the decimal equivalents for a penny, a nickel, a dime, a quarter, a half-dollar, and a dollar.

• Research-based Activity

Have learners make a list of items they would like to purchase at the grocery store. Once the lists have been made, take learners to the grocery store to research the prices of their selected items. Next, have learners find the sum of the prices to see how much they would spend in total.

• Test Prep

In this section, learners build a strong foundation in working with decimals. The following activities engage learners while preparing them for classroom testing in this area.

• Different Audiences

Have an accelerated learner keep a pretend bank account for a week. Have that learner write down any deductions he or she might make for purchases, as well as any deposits for money earned. Learners will gain valuable insight into real-world skills while working with decimals.

• Group Activity

Divide learners into a few large groups. Have each group open a store, selling classroom items. Give them fake money, both cash and coins, and arrange pens, pencils, paper, and other items for sale on several desks. Have learners take turns acting as the cashier, giving each person a chance to add up prices and make change.

Name _____

Comparing Decimals

Which Decimal Is Greater?

A decimal is a number with one or more digits to the right of the decimal point. The numbers to the left of the decimal point are whole numbers. The numbers to the right of the decimal point are fractions. The first number to the right of the decimal point is in the tenths place and the second number is in the hundredths place. We can use < (less than), > (greater than), and = (equal to) to show the relationship between two decimals.

Example: .34 is < 3.4

 Directions: Write >, <, or = in the box to complete each number phrase.

1. 3.9 [   ] .39   2. 1.8 [   ] 1.80

3. 1.9 [   ] 19   4. .23 [   ] 2.3

5. 2.61 [   ] 4.1   6. .981 [   ] 1.1

FUN FACT

The decimal system is believed to have been based on a system of counting on ten fingers.

41

Name _____

Line Up the Numbers

To add decimals, we line up the decimal points.	30.42
Example: To add 30.42 and 4.21, we line up the decimal points.	+ 4.21
	34.63

 Directions: Add the decimals below by lining up the decimal points in the space provided.

1. 1.62 + 4.38 = _____   2. 24.9 + 6.24 = _____

3. 8.1 + 1.05 = _____   4. 17.41 + 3.35 = _____

FUN FACT

Money values are written as decimals.

 = $.10

 = $.05

Name _____

Money Matters

To add or subtract decimals, we line up the decimal points.

Example: To subtract 9.07 – .46, we line up the decimal points.

$$\begin{array}{r} 9.07 \\ -.46 \\ \hline 8.61 \end{array}$$

 Directions: Solve the following word problems. Write your answers on the lines provided.

1. Mark had $30. He bought a pack of baseball cards that cost $1.05, a baseball cap that cost $15.78, and food that cost $4.29. How much money does Mark have left?

   _____

2. Rob brought three coupons with him to the grocery store to save money on his grocery bill. The coupons were for $.75 off, $1.25 off, and $3.50 off his total bill. If Rob's original total bill was for $86.13, what was his total bill after the coupon discounts?

   _____

3. Willem wants to buy 4 comic books. They cost $4.50, $2.99, $1.99, and $5.25. He has $12. Does Willem have enough money to buy the comics he wants?

   _____

4. Keisha got $40 for her birthday. She went to the toy store and bought a doll that cost $15.99, a game that cost $10.50, and a pack of stickers that cost $2.99. How much money does Keisha have left?

   _____

Name _____

Changing Decimals into Fractions

We can write decimals that have one digit to the right of the decimal point, in the tenths place, as fractions. The numerator is the digit in the tenths place. The denominator is 10.

Example: .3 = $\frac{3}{10}$

 Directions: Write each decimal as a fraction on the lines below.

1. 0.7 = _____

2. 0.1 = _____

3. 0.6 = _____

4. 0.2 = _____

5. 0.8 = _____

FUN FACT

Libraries use the Dewey Decimal System to classify books. Each book is assigned a decimal number so it can be found quickly.

44

Name _____

Skill Check—Decimals

Comparing Decimals

 Directions: Write >, <, or = in the box to complete the number sentence.

5.08 □ 50.01

Adding Decimals

 Directions: Solve the problem below by lining up the decimal points.

9.2 + 3.05 = _____

Decimal Word Problems

 Directions: Solve the problem below.

Jeff has $4.50. He wants to buy a bottle of water that costs $1.99, a granola bar that costs $.99, and a piece of chocolate that costs $0.25. How much money will Jeff have left after he buys everything he wants?

_____

Answer Key

p. 4
1. 426; 962; 5,691; 13,028
2. 219; 658; 9,720; 10,485
3. 397; 6,999; 7,509; 10,001
4. 868; 1,304; 8,091; 19,452

p. 5
1. 13,800
2. 2,000
3. 30,000
4. 9,080

p. 6
1. 1,867
2. 2,118
3. 3,007
4. 1,624

p. 7
1. 8 with a remainder of 1
2. 10 with a remainder of 1
3. 8 with a remainder of 1
4. 2 with a remainder of 5

p. 8
1. $\frac{3}{8}$ 2. $\frac{5}{8}$

3. $\frac{7}{8}$ 4. $\frac{2}{8}$ or $\frac{1}{4}$

p. 9
1. <
2. =
3. >
4. <

p. 11
1. 190; 782; 974; 1,236; 2,694
2. 294; 564; 985; 1,090; 1,468
3. 97; 512; 651; 2,012; 10,004
4. 396; 596; 1,678; 3,450;
    20,546

p. 12
Primes circled: 13 29 2 19 17
    11 19 3 7 5 31
Riddle answer:
    D I N N E R T A B L E

p. 13
1. C. 400 + 20 + 5
2. B. 5,000 + 900 + 6
3. B. 3,000 + 800 + 60 + 1
4. C. 10,000 + 2,000 + 300 + 8

p. 14
1. thirty-two
2. one hundred forty-five
3. six hundred four
4. one thousand one
    hundred sixty-five

p. 15
**Ordering and Comparing
    Numbers**
519; 983; 1,093; 10,211

Recognizing Prime Numbers
2, 11, and 13 should be
    circled.

Expanding Numbers
4,000 + 700 + 60 + 2

Numerals in Word Form
eight hundred forty-five
p. 17

1. five hundred thousand
2. five thousand
3. five million
4. fifty

p. 18
1. 3
2. 1
3. 8
4. 9

p. 19
1. 204,600
2. 5,000
3. 4,300,000
4. 490,620

p. 20
1. thousands
2. tens
3. ten thousands
4. hundreds

p. 21
Place Value
1. two hundred
2. 8

Rounding
1. 5,900
2. thousands

p. 23
1. 1,494
2. 2,382
3. 2,408
4. 3,003

p. 24
1. 586
2. 119
3. 141
4. 202

p. 25
1. yes
2. $17
3. 326
4. no

p. 26
1. yes
2. $502
3. no
4. $1,026

p. 27
Addition and Subtraction Problems
1. 1,369
2. 616

Addition and Subtraction Word Problems
1. 721
2. 69

p. 29
1. 1, 2, 4, 8, 16, 32
2. 3, 7, 9, and 12 should be circled
3. 1, 2, 4, 8, 16
4. 5, 9, and 10 should be circled

p. 30

	5	9	2	7	10
4	20	36	8	28	40
1	5	9	2	7	10
6	30	54	12	42	60
8	40	72	16	56	80
3	15	27	6	21	30
7	35	63	14	49	70
9	45	81	18	63	90
5	25	45	10	35	50
2	10	18	4	14	20

p. 31
1. 4 with a remainder of 4
2. 6 with a remainder of 1
3. 3 with a remainder of 1
4. 5 with a remainder of 1

p. 32
1. $45
2. Louis can fill 5 pages. He will have 3 cards left over.
3. 54
4. 4

p. 33
Recognizing Factors
3, 4, 8, 12, 2, 1, and 6 should be circled

Multiplication Tables

	0	8	5
11	0	88	55
4	0	32	20

Division with Remainders
1. 6 with a remainder of 1
2. 5 with a remainder of 2

p. 35
1. $\frac{2}{4}$ or $\frac{1}{2}$ 2. $1\frac{1}{4}$

3. $\frac{5}{8}$ 4. $\frac{5}{6}$

p. 36
Answers will vary.

p. 37
1. $\frac{7}{8}$ 2. $\frac{4}{5}$

3. $\frac{7}{16}$ 4. $\frac{10}{11}$

p. 38
1. $\frac{5}{8}$ 2. $\frac{3}{11}$

3. $\frac{5}{13}$ 4. $\frac{4}{9}$

p. 39
Identifying Representations
$\frac{3}{8}$

Equivalent Fractions
Answers will vary.

Fractions with Like Denominators
1. $\frac{7}{9}$

2. $\frac{3}{11}$

p. 41
1. >
2. =
3. <
4. <
5. <
6. <

p. 42
1. 6
2. 31.14
3. 9.15
4. 20.76

p. 43
1. $8.88
2. $80.63
3. no
4. $10.52

p. 44
1. $\frac{7}{10}$

2. $\frac{1}{10}$

3. $\frac{6}{10}$ or $\frac{3}{5}$

4. $\frac{2}{10}$ or $\frac{1}{5}$

5. $\frac{8}{10}$ or $\frac{4}{5}$

p. 45
Comparing Decimals
<

Adding Decimals
12.25

Decimal Word Problems
$1.27